SUPPORTING MUSLIM STUDENTS

A QUICK REFERENCE GUIDE FOR TEACHERS, TRAINERS & LECTURERS

SHEIKH MOHAMED ABDI DAHIR,
ANGUS DUNPHY, REVD DR PAUL FITZPATRICK,
DR SAJJAN M. GOHEL, HIFSA HAROON-IQBAL,
BARRIE PHILLIPS & SHAYKH DR ASIM

JOHN CATT
EDUCATIONAL
LIMITED

T0273317

First published 2017
by John Catt Educational Ltd,
12 Deben Mill Business Centre, Old Maltings Approach,
Melton, Woodbridge IP12 1BL
Tel: +44 (0) 1394 389850
Fax: +44 (0) 1394 386893
Email: enquiries@johncatt.com
Website: www.johncatt.com

ISBN: 978 1 911382 29 4

Set and designed by John Catt Educational Ltd
www.johncatt.com

Contents

Introduction

The purpose of the Quick Reference Guide is to equip teachers, trainers and lecturers with the fundamental knowledge and understanding to provide enhanced affective and cognitive support for their Muslim students – as well as providing all students with an additional reference for seeking clarification on issues of our/their time.

The guide can be used as a free-standing resource and/or as an integrated and complementary resource to the GOT Project. (See attached schema)

Need

The guide has been produced in response to an increasing number of requests from educational establishments (11 – 19 schools, Work Based Learning Providers, FE colleges and Higher Educational Institutions) to respond to issues concerning Muslim students as they go about their daily lives.

Context

The guide is the latest addition to the GOT (Getting On Together) Project, which seeks to counter all forms of extremism and promote tolerance and respect for all through the medium of school/college-based educational interventions and dedicated youth, community and adult workshops.

As such, it can claim to sit within – and complement – a family of products which have been funded and supported in part by Welsh Government and other benefactors over a period of several years.

Finally, the guide is not static and whilst core elements e.g. concerning faith will remain unalterable, it is expected that contexts will increase in response to changing circumstances, teachers' queries and its introduction into other sectors and places.

Indeed, the authors would welcome correspondence and suggestions regarding the inclusion of further advice and support that could be incorporated in subsequent editions – or through electronic, interactive routes.

N.B. The views and opinions presented in this guide are solely representative of those named authors below:

Authors

Sheikh Mohamed Abdi Dahir MA, imam, Noor-El-Islam mosque, Cardiff

Angus Dunphy OBE, former headteacher, trained inspector and education consultant

Dr Paul Fitzpatrick, chaplain-psychologist, Cardiff Metropolitan University

Dr Sajjan M. Gohel, International Security Director, Asia Pacific Foundation

Hifsa Haroon-Iqbal MBE DL Mphil, HE & FE Prevent Coordinator (West Midlands), Department for Education

Barrie Phillips, Project Director, The GOT Project; HE & FE Prevent Coordinator (Wales), Department for Education

Shaykh Dr Asim Yusuf, psychiatrist

Acknowledgements

We are indebted to Dr Wali Aslam, School of Politics, at the University of Surrey and Andrew Hobbs at RoHo Learning Ltd for their valuable insights and observations on the early draft document.

Also, to the Muslim Council of Wales for providing important counter narratives to facilitate further discussion and adaptions on key religious and political issues.

Our grateful thanks extend to the following who proof read the final draft with vigour:

Shreya Das, Fellow at the South Asia Democratic Forum

Charlotte A. Jordan, Researcher

Katie Louise Pearce, MSc Graduate History of International Relations at LSE

Kritika Singh, Student/Researcher

Jacqueline R. Sutherland, Counter-Terrorism Research Fellow, the Asia-Pacific Foundation.

Gill Vaisey, Religious Education Consultant, whose extensive knowledge and understanding clarified and guided our responses to key contextual scenarios.

Finally, our unstinting appreciation extends to school, WBL, college and university staff, who illuminated our purpose with their wish to better understand Muslim students as well as core issues and events of our time.

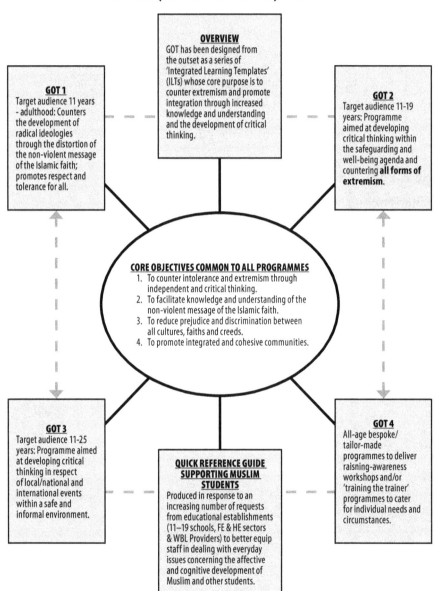

SCHEMA
THE GOT (GETTING ON TOGETHER) PROJECT

OVERVIEW
GOT has been designed from the outset as a series of 'Integrated Learning Templates' (ILTs) whose core purpose is to counter extremism and promote integration through increased knowledge and understanding and the development of critical thinking.

GOT 1
Target audience 11 years - adulthood: Counters the development of radical ideologies through the distortion of the non-violent message of the Islamic faith; promotes respect and tolerance for all.

GOT 2
Target audience 11-19 years: Programme aimed at developing critical thinking within the safeguarding and well-being agenda and countering **all forms of extremism**.

CORE OBJECTIVES COMMON TO ALL PROGRAMMES
1. To counter intolerance and extremism through independent and critical thinking.
2. To facilitate knowledge and understanding of the non-violent message of the Islamic faith.
3. To reduce prejudice and discrimination between all cultures, faiths and creeds.
4. To promote integrated and cohesive communities.

GOT 3
Target audience 11-25 years: Programme aimed at developing critical thinking in respect of local/national and international events within a safe and informal environment.

QUICK REFERENCE GUIDE SUPPORTING MUSLIM STUDENTS
Produced in response to an increasing number of requests from educational establishments (11–19 schools, FE & HE sectors & WBL Providers) to better equip staff in dealing with everyday issues concerning the affective and cognitive development of Muslim and other students.

GOT 4
All-age bespoke/tailor-made programmes to deliver raisning-awareness workshops and/or 'training the trainer' programmes to cater for individual needs and circumstances.

THE GOT (GETTING ON TOGETHER) PROJECT

GOT 1

Target audience 11 years – adulthood:
Counters the development of radical ideologies through the distortion of the non-violent message of the Islamic faith; promotes respect and tolerance for all.

GOT 2

Target audience 11-19 years:
Programme aimed at developing critical thinking within the safeguarding and well-being agenda and countering all forms of extremism. Incorporated within the Welsh Baccalaureate September 2015 and accredited by WJEC Examination Board.

GOT 3

Target audience 11-25 years:
Facilitates self-exploration and rationalisation of thoughts and feelings around extremism and intolerance in today's society within a safe and informal environment using the NAOMIE template. Incorporated within a Level 3 programme and accredited by AgoredCymru for the Third Sector.

GOT 4

All-age bespoke/tailor-made programmes to deliver raising-awareness workshops and/or 'training the trainer' programmes to cater for individual needs and circumstances. Delivered to e.g. adult communities and professional groups

OVERVIEW

GOT has been designed from the outset as a series of 'Integrated Learning Templates (ILTs) whose core purpose is to counter extremism and promote integration through increased knowledge and understanding and the development of critical thinking.

CORE OBJECTIVES COMMON TO ALL PROGRAMMES

1. To counter intolerance and extremism through independent and critical thinking.
2. To facilitate knowledge and understanding of the non-violent message of the Islamic faith.
3. To reduce prejudice and discrimination between all cultures, faiths and creeds.
4. To promote integrated and cohesive communities.

QUICK REFERENCE GUIDE: SUPPORTING MUSLIM STUDENTS

Produced in response to an increasing number of requests from educational establishments (11–19 schools, Work Based Learning Providers, FE and HE sectors) to better equip staff in dealing with everyday issues concerning the affective and cognitive development of Muslim and non-Muslim students.

Foreword

During a ministry spanning five decades, I have engaged with tens of thousands of people, each with their own distinct view on the subject of God, which has enriched, corroborated, challenged and formed my own view. The strength of this wide-ranging pocket guide is that it will enable such dialogue rather than close conversation down. Based on the principle of respect for deeply held faith and practice, it seeks to provide non-Muslims with some pointers on how to manage the interface between the sacred and the secular, to the mutual benefit of both. There are clear guidelines where the rules which order the common life of a school or college should have a priority which is eminently reasonable, as well as giving instances where gracious hospitality to a student's faith-needs can enable well-being and flourishing.

One of the many things shared by the three Abrahamic religions is that faith is a journey shaped by the myriad fellow-travellers encountered en-route. Education too is about a journey, from darkness to light, from prejudice to understanding. All too often we begin at a squalid base camp, where we bolster our insecurity by making ourselves look big by belittling others; education enables us to rise above that, to rejoice in difference and the colour it brings to our otherwise monochrome world. One of the many strengths of this book is that it portrays a Muslim community which itself is multi-coloured rather than monochrome, with the concomitant danger of treating Islam as monolith rather than multi-layered. For me as a Christian, God at heart is Love, a Love which spends itself by being impaled on his suffering creation, a Love which is hurting in every wounded child and seeks healing. This pocket-guide, openly and objectively, surveys the wounds suffered nationally and internationally over the last century, within and outside the Muslim community, encouraging a tenderness with each other's hurts, as well as an honouring of each other as cherished children of God.

Rt Rev'd David Wilbourne
Esgob Cynorthwyol Llandaf
Assistant Bishop of Llandaff and Director of Ministry

11

1. BACKGROUND TO ISLAM

(A) ISLAM

1. What does the word Islam mean?

Linguistically Islam has two meanings:

a) Peace – When Muslims meet they greet each other by saying 'Assalaamu Alaykum' (Peace be upon you). Please note that 'As-Salaam' is one of the proper names of Allah, Almighty God. (Noble Qur'an. Surah 59: al-Hashr, 23)

b) Submission – To the will of Allah, the Almighty God.

In short, Islam means to achieve peace through the devotion to the will of Allah, the Almighty God. (N.B. Allah is the Arabic word for God; see point 12)

A practising Muslim strives to submit wholeheartedly to God, therefore fulfilling his commitment to achieve peace in this life and the next.

2. Is Islam one of the Abrahamic religions and if so what does this mean?

Like Judaism and Christianity it is one of the Abrahamic religions. This means that all prophets and messengers who came after Abraham were of his line (offspring) – for example prophets like Isaac, Ismael, Jacob, Moses, Jesus, Muhammad, Peace Be Upon Him (PBUH), are his offspring. This means it is a religion based on revelation – guidance given by God to the prophets for all nations. (Qur'an 3:84). (Note – Islam begins with Adam).

13

3. Who can give me a ruling on Islamic matters?

A recognised scholar, or sheikh who holds an ijazah (an authorisation to minister, guide and teach), will be able to do this. The ijazah testifies that the holder has acquired expert knowledge of Islam after many years of study and learning from and with Islamic scholars. But these experts must derive their rulings from the Sunnah (see point 14) and the Qur'an (Koran) (see point 15) as understood and practised by the immediate students of Prophet Muhammad (PBUH) – the Companions.

(B) BELIEFS

4. What are the fundamental beliefs that should be held by all Muslims?

All Muslims base their beliefs on:
- Five pillars of Islam
- Six articles of faith
- Ihsan

These are called the Three Layers of Islam. All who adhere to these three layers are recognised as upstanding and faithful to their religion and are expected to be tolerant, peaceful and respectful to all. These layers are explained in the sections which follow.

(C) THE FIVE PILLARS OF ISLAM

5. What are the five pillars of Islam?

There are five pillars of Islam which are central to the 'Worship of Allah/Almighty God in the religion.' The majority of Islamic law and guidance actually relates to inter-personal ethics, in family, societal, financial and other dimensions.

The five pillars are:
- Shahadah – the declaration of faith;
- Salah – performing five daily prayers;
- Sawm – fasting during the Holy month of Ramadan;

1. Background to Islam

- Zakah – giving charity in accordance with your wealth; and
- Hajj – making a pilgrimage to Makkah (Mecca) at least once in your lifetime (subject to health, wealth and personal safety).

Apart from their ritual significance, they have deep symbolic resonances with the human relationship to God, creation, themselves and life.

6. What is Shahadah (Testimony)?

A Muslim is expected to declare their faith by saying, 'There is no object of worship other than Allah/Almighty God and Muhammad (PBUH) His messenger.'

A Muslim believes that the only purpose of life is to serve and obey God and this is done by following the example of Muhammad (PBUH), the messenger.

Shahada represents a reaffirmation that one's ultimate purpose is a relationship with God.

7. What is Salah (Five Daily Prayers)?

Prayers are offered five times each day as a duty towards Allah. Their purpose is to bring God to mind, purify the heart and prevent temptation. Male Muslims are expected to perform these, when possible, in the mosque as a congregation. Female Muslims are free to pray wherever it is most convenient. The timings of the prayers are the same however, for males and females. Prayer times are approximately at dawn to just before sunrise; midday (around 12.00 – 2.00 p.m. during winter and 1.30 – 4.00 p.m. in the summer); late afternoon, sunset and approximately two hours after sunset. Midday Friday prayer is the most important prayer of the week and one of the three Eids mentioned by the prophet Muhammad (PBUH). It is a non-fasting day unless you fast a day before or a day after. Some Muslims consider it forbidden (according to Allah) to fast for only one day if it is Friday or Saturday because Friday is the day of Du'aa', Dhikr and worship. (Sahih ibn Khuzaimah. Vol 3, 315, 2161)

Note: Times will vary across the UK. Check with your local mosque. (See point 62) The act of ritual prayer serves as a reconnection of the believer to Allah/God Almighty and a reminder of one's ultimate origin and end.

8. What is Sawm (Fasting)?

Fasting is carried out during the holy month of Ramadan. Muslims abstain from food and water during the hours from sunrise to sunset and are expected to refrain from intercourse. Ramadan aims to encourage love, sincerity and devotion, and to develop patience, will-power and selflessness. In so doing, it promotes respect and tolerance for others and discourages telling lies and speaking ill of people (backbiting). It also helps the wealthy to empathise with the difficulties faced by those who suffer from hunger.

The ill, elderly and prepubescent are exempt from fasting, but may use their personal choice and decide to fast.

Fasting represents the need to spiritually discipline oneself and abstain from the worst aspects of human nature.

9. What is Zakah (Purification of Wealth)?

Those Muslims who can afford it are required as a religious duty to give alms, for example, money or animals (camels, sheep, goats, cattle). Those who give money are expected to give 2.5% of their net savings. The sum is to be spent directly on those who are entitled, such as the poor. Muslims are required to help the poor, orphans and the needy etc. wherever possible (Noble Qur'an 9:60) and to share their opportunities with those less fortunate than themselves.

Zakat represents the nature of a Muslim's interaction with creation, which is based on selflessness, compassion and assistance.

10. What is Hajj (Pilgrimage to Makkah)?

Muslims have a duty to go on a pilgrimage to Makkah at least once in their lifetime if they can afford it and if health and personal safety permit. Three million Muslims, from all races and from across the world, make the pilgrimage to the sacred city of Makkah in Saudi Arabia, each year. They progress to the house of Allah, the Ka'bah. This is an ancient cube shaped building dating from Abraham's time.

Muslims walk around it seven times on their Hajj anti-clockwise as part of their pilgrimage ritual, starting from the Black Stone.

Hajj represents the reality of life, which is a journey through life to find God, that all people must undergo

(D) THE SIX ARTICLES OF FAITH

11. What are the six articles of faith?

These are the fundamentals of the faith which every Muslim must adhere to without a shred of doubt. They include belief in Allah, His angels, His books, His messengers, the hereafter and in predestination. The following asterisked (*) sections deal with these in greater detail.

*12. What do Muslims believe about Allah?

A Muslim believes in one God, who is merciful and the sole creator and sustainer of the universe. They use the Arabic name for God – 'Allah'. Muslims believe that Allah has infinite wisdom and knowledge. Allah is all-powerful and knows what is happening everywhere in His creation. Allah is not indifferent to the world. He is wise, just and loving. A Muslim believes that sometimes a human being fails to understand His wisdom but accepts that there is wisdom and purpose behind everything.

*13. Do Muslims believe in Angels?

Muslims believe that Allah created the angels. They cannot commit sins and have no gender. Different angels have different responsibilities. For example, the Archangel Gabriel – who is an angel messenger of Allah – brought Allah's commands to all human prophets and messengers such as Abraham, Noah, Moses, Jesus and Muhammad (PBUH). These messengers in Islam are called the Messengers of Strong Will (Noble Qur'an. Surah 46:35)

14. What are the Sunnah and Hadith?

Sunnah: This is the totality of the Way of Life of the prophet Muhammad (PBUH) which Muslims are obliged to follow. Sunnah is sometimes described as the Prophet's character.

Hadith: Linguistically this means 'information'. In practice, Hadith refers to the sayings, actions, approvals and/or disapprovals of the prophet Muhammed (PBUH).

A hadith consists of a body of text and a chain of transmission by which the statement's authenticity may be assessed. Muslims place a heavy emphasis on verifying the statement, as well as understanding it, before acting upon it.

*15. What are the Holy Books?

Muslims believe that the following four books were revealed by Allah and are therefore divine:

(a) The first book was the Torah which was revealed to Moses.

(b) The second book is Zabuur (the psalms of David).

(c) The third book is Injeel (Gospel) which was revealed to Jesus.

(d) The fourth book, the Qur'an (Koran), Muslims believe encapsulates all the previous messages and supersedes the previous three books

The Qur'an contains the final words of Allah and is the pillar of the Muslim faith. The Qur'an was revealed to the last prophet, Muhammad (PBUH), through the Archangel Gabriel, over a period of 23 years. The Qur'an, Muslims believe, confirms and finalises all of the revelations that had been passed down to humans. The word Qur'an means 'recitation' and Muslims are expected to learn it and follow its guidelines.

Muslims believe that the Qur'an is the greatest miracle which proves the prophethood of Muhammad (PBUH), because he was unlettered and because of the matchless eloquence it demonstrates. Muslims also believe the Qur'an gives the true meaning of Allah's message, rather than relying totally upon the books of God which preceded it, which may have been altered or misunderstood over the course of time. In order to understand the Qur'an you have to use the authentic sayings and actions of the Prophet, together with a sound knowledge of the Arabic language and the application of the Qur'an by His immediate students called Sahabah (Companions).

A surah is a chapter of the Holy Book. The Holy Qur'an has 114 surahs. Every surah but one begins with the words, "In the name of Allah, the Compassionate, the Merciful."

*16. Do Muslims believe in messengers?

Muslims believe that Allah sent his messengers and prophets to all people. Muslims accept prophets mentioned in the Qur'an, including Noah, Abraham, Muhammed (PBUH), Adam, Ishmael, Isaac, Moses, David and Jesus. They believe that the prophets were human beings chosen as examples for humankind and also to teach and guide them to the right path. Muslims believe that denying/rejecting any of the prophets means rejection of Allah. Muslims believe that none of them has divinity. They are all honoured servants of Allah.

17. What is the difference between a prophet and a messenger?

According to Muslims a messenger is a prophet who receives new revelations and laws from Allah so that he conveys that message to the people, e.g. Abraham, Muhammad (PBUH), Noah, Moses, Jesus. A prophet is someone who is made responsible by Allah to revive existing revelations so he teaches and guides people according to existing revelations and laws.

18. What do Muslims believe about Jesus?

Muslims believe he is one of the greatest prophets and messengers and they respect him. They believe in the virgin birth, his miraculous abilities and the sainthood of Mary. Jesus is mentioned in the Qur'an many times. He is closest in time to Muhammad (PBUH).

**19. Do Muslims believe in The Resurrection and what do Muslims believe about sin?

Yes. A Muslim believes in the last day of reckoning and in keeping faith with Allah throughout life on earth. A Muslim believes that humans are born without sin and that each person is responsible during their lifetime for their own actions and behaviour. No one is expected to bear the burden of others (Qur'an 6:164). All are expected to seek the guidance of Allah and to keep their heart pure. Only Allah can grant salvation, which is a pure gift from God, but one becomes worthy of it by doing good (This is defined by Muslims as a) doing what Allah says and b) refraining from doing what Allah prohibits.) You cannot inherit salvation – you must earn it through putting your beliefs into actions.

20. Ihsan

Ihsan is defined as worshipping God as though you are seeing Him, but if you are not able to, then being conscious that He sees you. It also means excellence and beauty of conduct. It relates to one's internal state of awe and devotion rather than merely performing the outward action 'robotically.'

That means whatever you intend, whatever you say, whatever you do He is aware of and must be according to His will. So we must achieve excellence in everything.

(E) MUHAMMAD (PBUH)
(Full name: Muhammad, son of Abdullah, son of Abd al-Muttalib, from the clan of Hashim and the tribe of Quraysh.)

21. Who is he?

He was born in 570 AD to a noble family in Makkah (Mecca). Muhammad means 'praised one'. He was orphaned at an early age. He was looked after by his grandfather (Abdulmuttalib) and then his uncle (Abu- Talib). He became known as Al-Amin, which means 'the trusted one'. Even before Islam, Muhammad (PBUH) was interested in the problems of his society.

At the age of forty he received his first revelation from Allah, during the ninth month of the lunar calendar, Ramadan. The message was delivered by the Angel Gabriel. It said 'Recite in the name of your Lord who created man from a seed. Recite! For your Lord is most bountiful; He taught by the Pen that which man knew not.' So Muhammad (PBUH) started to teach the people.

Over the next twenty three years he continued to receive revelations. The messages from the Qur'an and his traditions (Hadith) are for all humanity. The first believer was his wife Khadijah – whom he married when he was 25 and she 40 – who is respected as the mother of Muslims.

The citizens of Makkah (Mecca) increasingly saw Muhammad (PBUH) as a threat as he forbade the worship of idols and called for support of the weak.

In 622 AD Allah told Muhammad (PBUH) to leave Makkah and go to the northern city of Medina. Here he built the first Muslim society. Eight years later he led 10,000 men back to Makkah, with orders that not a single drop of blood was to be spilt. The rulers of Makkah submitted without a fight and the majority accepted Islam. Muhammad (PBUH) died in 632 AD and was buried in Medina.

22. What is a mosque?

It is highly recommended for all Muslim men to pray in a mosque. However, if a Muslim cannot make it to the mosque, a Muslim can pray in any clean space. Muhammad (PBUH) said, 'The whole earth is a mosque'.

A mosque is a building whose main purpose is set aside for offering daily prayer to Allah. Traditionally, a mosque consists of a domed building and a minaret from which the faithful are called to prayer (these days, usually from loudspeakers set high up on the structure). The man who calls the men to pray is called the Mu'azzin. Inside the mosque there is just a simple space, where men pray together, facing Makkah. The direction of Makkah is often signified by a simple niche (Mihrab).

Ostentatious decorations are discouraged because it is considered distracting from prayer. Friday prayer is the most important prayer service of the week and men are expected to attend. It is not obligatory for women, but many do, usually taking up their positions in a screened off part or behind men to avoid distractions from the religious purpose.

At the Friday service the Imam recites a verse/verses from the Qur'an. The choice of verse/verses will be linked to a message/sermon.

2. GUIDANCE FOR SCHOOL/ COLLEGE STAFF

(F) RAMADAN

23. What is Ramadan and when does it occur?

Muslims fast from dawn to dusk in the holy month of Ramadan, which lasts for 29/30 days according to the lunar calendar. It is the ninth month in the Muslim calendar. As it is calculated on the phases of the moon the date of Ramadan varies or moves each year. Schools and examination boards should be aware of its timing within any given year and plan accordingly to meet Muslim pupils' needs.

24. How might a school support its Muslim children during Ramadan?

In most, if not all schools with a population of Muslim pupils, pupils will fast. Schools will therefore wish to help and support their students. Staff should note that fasting may make individuals feel weak and pupils may take a little longer with their thought processes. PE staff should be especially considerate at this time.

25. What happens if a child is fasting but is entitled to a free school meal?

Schools will wish to be supportive and considerate to those of their pupils who fast during the holy month of Ramadan. Some schools have 'doggy bags' available, made up to the value of the free school meal, which pupils can take at lunch time if they wish and eat at home after sunset.

Parents and the mosque should be contacted to explain how the school is trying to support their children, before this measure is introduced.

With regard to primary school children who are fasting in school hours, the school should ensure that this is with the knowledge of the parent/guardian.

26. In what circumstances would a pupil not fast?

For example, in the case of pre-pubescent pupils they are not required to fast. However, some pupils – with the backing of their parents – may choose to fast or partly fast during the school day.

(G) EID

27. What is Eid?

There are two main Eid festivals in the year. Both are important:
(1) Eid-ul-Fitr – Festival of the breaking of the fast at the end of Ramadan (Little Eid), and
(2) Eid-ul-Adha – Occurs during the time of the Hajj (pilgrimage to Makkah). Families attend the mosque for special services in the morning and then celebrate with, for example, special meals. Presents are often given. This Eid is known as the festival of sacrifice and commemorates the Prophet Abraham's willingness to sacrifice his son for God. Pupils often refer to this as 'Big Eid'.

28. Will Muslim pupils attend school at Eid?

Regulations concerning school attendance in respect of religious observance are available from respective government departments. Schools should refer to these regulations to ascertain what constitutes permitted/authorised absences and their recording

As this is a day, or sometimes two, of religious observance attendance is not likely. Schools need to be sensitive to days of religious observance. In practice, schools will find it helpful to consult the local mosque and by building a productive relationship, agree to a pattern of leave for religious observance. Both school and mosque can inform young people what is expected of them in relation to school attendance. In this way unauthorised absences can more effectively be chased up. Since Eid falls according to the lunar calendar – with the possibility that the exact day may not be known until the day before – schools need to be flexible.

(H) *JIHAD

29. What exactly is the meaning of jihad?

N.B. Jihad does not mean 'holy war'. The term 'holy war' (Al-Harbu Al-Muqaddasatu in Arabic) does not appear in Islamic teachings.

Jihad means 'struggle' or 'exertion' and has many forms.

Note: In a curriculum pilot on challenging extremism funded by Welsh Assembly Government in 2009 the true meaning of jihad was shown to be misunderstood by 300 Muslim and non-Muslim KS4 students. This lack of understanding represents a serious concern for young and old alike when dealing with alternative (false and/or violent) interpretations. Jihad has been divided by classical scholars into thirteen categories of struggle comprising four key areas:

- struggle against self
- struggle against satan
- struggle against disbelief
- struggle against criminality

Only one of these thirteen struggles relates to conflict, fighting or war:

(a) Internal struggle (this has been called 'the greatest jihad'): one meaning of jihad is the internal struggle to resist what you know to be wrong – and the internal struggle to do the right thing, such as respecting your parents and working hard in school. This meaning applies to all – Muslims and non-Muslims.

One particularly praised form of jihad is 'speaking truth to power', or standing up as a moral voice for the weak and oppressed in a positive and peaceful way. The Prophet said, "the best jihad is to speak the truth to a tyrant."

(b) Offensive jihad – Conditions★:
- Only strong, Islamic governments can conduct offensive

jihad. That is, jihad follows a declaration of war between two warring nations/empires/a state with a standing army. This political warfare becomes jihad if done in accordance with the moral teachings of Islam.

- Individuals or groups are not allowed to use offensive jihad as a means to stop what they perceive to be atrocities or wrongdoing.
- Offensive jihad does not mean the killing of innocent men, women or children.
- Offensive jihad does not allow the destruction of buildings, infrastructure or transport.

(c) Defensive jihad – Conditions*:

- Defensive jihad means that law-abiding individuals, groups and governments have the right to use force if attacked.
- Defensive jihad is legal both in Islamic law and international law. But, whether actions are claimed to be offensive or defensive jihad:
    - Jihad is NOT killing innocent civilians – men, women and children such as happened for example in Mumbai 2008, the Twin Towers ('9/11') atrocity, Charlie Hebdo and Bataclan attacks in Paris 2015, Berlin 2016, London in March 2017 and elsewhere.
    - Jihad is NOT killing elderly people.
    - Jihad is NOT killing religious people (priests, monks, nuns, vicars, etc).
    - Jihad is NOT destroying public transport and infrastructure and innocent lives, such as happened to the London bus and tube trains on 7/7.
    - Jihad is NOT taking your own life, such as suicide bombings – Islam absolutely forbids this.
    - Jihad is NOT actively searching out and killing e.g. foreign soldiers and others. What is called 'guerrilla war' is categorically NOT supported by Islam.

ANY ACT AS THOSE DESCRIBED ABOVE IS NOT JIHAD BUT TERRORISM AND MURDER
*Taken from GOT 2 – 11-19 Challenging Extremism

(I) SCHOOL MEALS

30. How adaptable do school meals have to be?

Remember that the pupil is the client. At the very least pupils should be aware of the school menus and where dishes contain pork they should be clearly labelled. A school kitchen should offer a variety of foods, which allows choices to be made by each of the school communities involved. Some authorities provide halal meals. These are meals that have been prepared following the rules of the faith (e.g. the way animals are slaughtered, the absence of pork which is forbidden (Haram) etc). Accommodation and supervision for those wishing to bring their own food must be provided by schools.

(J) SCHOOL DRESS CODE

31. Does the school dress code support the needs of its pupils?

Governors are responsible for drawing up a school policy regarding dress code. It should meet the needs of its families. Supportive policies take into consideration family circumstances and ethnic and religious needs. These needs may vary between different cultural/ethnic groups from the same religious background. Many schools' policies allow Muslim girls (and others if they so wish) to wear both a plain headscarf and the Shalwar Kameez – a top and baggy trousers favoured by e.g. Punjabi women. Different forms of modest dress are also worn by people from other cultures. However, these usually have to be in school colours. It is essential therefore, when drawing up policies, to engage with parents, students, the local mosque and the local authority. This gains maximum community support and understanding and allows schools to discipline transgressors, whilst avoiding conflict.

32. Should I let a Muslim girl pupil leave my lesson to adjust her headscarf if asked?

Yes. A headscarf protects the modesty of a Muslim girl. However, she may well be able to adjust her scarf in a less public part of the room without leaving. Repeated requests to do this are unacceptable and the student should be informed of pending contact with the year head/home/mosque on grounds of classroom disruption. In all cases it should be made clear that pupils are expected to enter the lesson prepared both in mind and dress. One colleague who worked in a madrassa said the possibility of a headscarf loosening was overcome by introducing a simple standardised headscarf as part of the uniform which did not require constant adjustment .

33. Can a Muslim girl come to school with her face covered with a niqab or burka?

A burka covers the whole body including all of the face and the eyes (a gauze is sewn in so that the wearer can see). A niqab is a face veil but it does not cover the eyes. It is not usual for Muslim girls in British schools to wear these garments. If allowance is not made in the governors' uniform policy then it is not allowed.

Note:

(1) The governors' dress code policy will determine what can be worn.

(2) However, schools are strongly advised to work with the parents and local communities to meet local needs. Schools are advised to make sure parents are issued annually with the school's uniform requirements.

Many Muslims choose not to wear the niqab or burka (or the hijab), but the Qur'an requires all students to display modesty in their dress. Schools should also have dress code policies for their staff, which are regularly issued and freely available.

34. What happens if dress impedes safety?

It is the duty of the school and its staff to operate safe practices. There are already well tried and tested measures for ensuring pupil safety in subjects like PE, DT and Science. The existing safety procedures should be used. Specific difficulties should be reported to senior management. The best schools and teachers have always found ways around any specific difficulty, whilst still protecting pupils' safety. Teachers and others should be careful to avoid confrontation and they should be proactive in reporting and resolving difficulties. Under no circumstances must a child be told to take off a garment (except for outer coat as they come into school from outside).

35. Do Muslim pupils need to wear jewellery for faith purposes?

Islam, as a religion, does not demand or recommend any jewellery or the decoration of any part of the body in public. However, cultural practices may involve the decorating/painting of e.g. hands and wrists.

All schools should have policies regarding the wearing of jewellery. These should be regularly communicated to pupils, parents and staff. It is helpful if the local mosque is aware of the policy. Many schools allow limited jewellery. Some Muslim girls paint their hands/wrists with henna patterns particularly on special occasions. In these cases a school may decide to be sensitive to a community's culture.

(K) SUBJECTS IN THE SCHOOL CURRICULUM

36. Can Muslim girl pupils take part in swimming lessons?

Pupils have to take part in the National Curriculum and therefore must take swimming lessons if they are part of the PE curriculum. However, wherever possible, schools need to be sensitive to the requirement of the Muslim faith to dress modestly. Schools can easily allow girls to cover their legs by wearing tracksuit bottoms. There are also modesty-preserving full-body swimsuits (Burkhinis) that are widely available. One secondary school with a swimming pool on site had the pool building windows painted to a height of eight feet so that boys could not look in. The local community was reassured.

In respect of mixed-sex swimming lessons, schools should consult with their local education department to ensure sensitive and sensible application of agreed procedures.

N.B. Some Muslim boys may request they wear knee-length shorts for PE/swimming to comply with rules around modesty in Islamic teachings.

37. Can Muslim girls refuse to wear shorts for PE?

As Muslim girls are taught in the home to act with modesty most schools allow girls to wear tracksuits for a range of PE activities if they so wish.

38. Must Muslim girls do cross country running?

If it is part of the PE curriculum then the answer is yes. However, as all activities are supervised, female PE staff will be out on the course with the girls.

39. Can Key stage 4 option PE (examination course, 14-16) be mixed sex?

As pupils have a choice whether or not to choose this subject, then the answer is yes. However, it should be plainly stated in all option literature sent to parents and given to pupils that the groups will be mixed sex.

40. Do Muslim pupils have to study music and (where it is part of the school curriculum) drama up to the end of key stage 3?

Yes. The school should make all parents aware of National Curriculum requirements and any additions it offers through its prospectus. Be aware that some Muslim parents believe that listening to and playing music goes against Islamic teaching whilst others would not agree with them. However, parents do not have the right to withdraw their children from music lessons in the National Curriculum.

41. Can I teach the theory of evolution in science in order to deliver the syllabus?

Yes. A teacher's duty is to teach the full syllabus and adequately prepare a pupil for assessment. Where examination preparation is concerned teachers may well use model answers to reinforce learning. Remember that you are not questioning an individual's belief. This must at all times be respected. However some examination questions will require a student to provide a Darwinian answer. Pupils should be advised to answer the question, so that they gain maximum marks. However there is nothing stopping them from declaring afterwards that they disagree with Darwin on faith grounds. If they do this they should leave a line or two between the exam answer and their personal statement. As marking is based on what a pupil knows this will not hinder them.

42. Do Muslim pupils have to undertake PSE/PSHE?

Yes. PSHE is part of the basic curriculum of schools and they will be aware of government frameworks and guidelines. Schools should ensure that all parents, whether Muslim or not, are aware of course content. Good schools are able to build parental confidence through the sensitive teaching of such topics as sex education and drug/alcohol education.

In Wales, primary schools are not legally required to provide sex education, but many choose to do so. The Governing Body of a secondary maintained school is required to see that a written statement of their policy is kept, with copies freely available to parents.

In England, at the time of writing, it looks as if primary schools will be required to include sex education in their curriculum. Parents have the right to withdraw their child from sex education lessons.

In Islam sexual relationships outside of marriage are prohibited (Haram), as is the case in Christianity and Judaism.

43. Should I allow pupil discussion in PSHE lessons on arranged marriage?

Certainly, if it is part of the syllabus. If effective teaching and learning is a feature of the school, pupils will have learnt to listen to each other and respect each other's point of view, without necessarily agreeing. Some Muslims will have their marriage arranged for them by parents. The marriage will be discussed by the family, and bride and groom will be part of that discussion. In the marriage ceremony itself a bride and groom may not be in the same room when the vows are taken.

Note that Islam prohibits that parents force their daughters or sons into a marriage they don't want. The following command of the Prophet is one of the most rigorously authenticated hadiths in the Islamic tradition, from a work called Bukhari:

'No woman, whether previously married or unmarried, shall be married without her consent.'

44. Do Muslim pupils have to study RE?

Religious education is a curriculum subject which schools must provide for all registered pupils at the school from Reception class to, and including, Post-16. Welsh Government, through its *National exemplar framework for religious education 3 to 19-year-olds in Wales*, suggests that pupils in a Nursery or Nursery class have a non-statutory entitlement to religious education.

Every Local Authority has an Agreed Syllabus for RE which is the statutory curriculum document for all Maintained and Voluntary Controlled Schools within that Authority. All Agreed Syllabuses for RE in Wales have taken into account the guidance offered by the above framework in order to ensure much commonality of requirements across local authorities. Religious education in Faith Schools is determined by the trust deed or the religious tenets of the school.

Each of the twenty two LAs in Wales has a Standing Advisory Council on Religious Education (SACRE) – a local committee of representatives of teachers' associations, local churches and faith groups, and the local authority (see Welsh Government Circular 10/94), which advises on religious education according to the local Agreed Syllabus. (In England see Circular 1/94). The Education Act 1996 Section 375 (3) states that RE in schools is required to reflect 'the religious traditions which in Britain are in the main Christian, whilst taking account of the teachings and practices of other principal religions represented in Great Britain'. (Circular 10/94)

One of the categories of representation on the SACRE includes Christian denominations and other religions, the number of whose representatives shall, 'so far as is consistent with the efficient discharge of the committee's functions, reflect broadly the proportionate strength of that denomination or religion in the area'. As a consequence, there may be a representative from the Islamic faith on the committee.

Religious education according to an Agreed Syllabus for RE, is an objective study, exploration and consideration of the beliefs, teachings and practices of people in local, national and global communities. Religious education provides pupils with the opportunity to develop an understanding of different people's beliefs and how those beliefs are practised in everyday life. Religious education encourages pupils to reflect on their learning and form and express their own views and opinions about their own and others' lifestyles. Studies in religious

31

education will help pupils develop a more informed understanding of current issues and world events associated with religion and belief and develop a more discerning and critical approach to media news coverage.

Religious education is not about indoctrinating or nurturing children into a faith or promoting any particular belief system. Religious education should not be confused with collective worship which is a different and distinct aspect of the school's wider provision.

Religious education as a classroom subject will, however, make a significant contribution to pupils' spiritual, moral, social and cultural development. It will play a major role in supporting children in becoming ethical, informed citizens.

Any parent/guardian has the right to request the withdrawal of their child(ren) wholly or partly from RE. WASACRE (the Wales Association of Standing Advisory Councils on Religious Education) has produced guidance on *Managing the Right of Withdrawal from RE* (2017) and this will provide a useful resource for any schools who receive requests from parents to withdraw their child(ren) from religious education.

Through open and honest discussion about the aims of the curriculum, the content of schemes of work and the learning intentions of individual class teachers, often parents who might have raised concerns will be reassured and appreciate the value of objective religious education for their child(ren) and support their inclusion in lessons.

(L) THE DAILY ACT OF COLLECTIVE WORSHIP

45. Do Muslim pupils have to attend the daily act of collective worship (DACW)?

Schools must provide collective worship daily for all registered pupils at a school except those in Nursery classes. In Maintained schools, most acts of collective worship in each term should be wholly or mainly of a broadly Christian character. This means that they should reflect the broad traditions of Christian belief without being distinctive of any particular Christian denomination. Within this there is room, on occasion, to deliver collective worship which will reflect the beliefs, texts and practices of other faiths. However, collective worship should take account of the family backgrounds, ages and aptitudes of the pupils involved.

School acts of collective worship are educationally meaningful when they provide opportunities to engage with the needs of all learners, whatever their faith or belief background. Good collective worship promotes spiritual development, contributes to personal development, benefits the whole school community, links the school community and the wider local community, and enhances awareness of global citizenship.

Those leading collective worship should be sensitive to the range of beliefs held by pupils in the school. Collective worship should give pupils the opportunity to worship without encouraging them to do something that is against the teachings of their religion. For example, times of prayer may be left open-ended for pupils to say their own prayers silently.

A parent / guardian can request that their child is excused from collective worship and schools must agree to such requests. Parents do not have to give reasons for requesting that their child is withdrawn from collective worship. Pupils who are excused must be supervised by the school. The school may, in agreement with parents, provide alternative arrangements for worship for one or more pupils that are excused, but is not obliged to do so. The school prospectus should refer to parents' right to request that their child is excused from collective worship and outline the arrangements for pupils who are excused.

The Education and Inspections Bill 2006 gives pupils in sixth forms the right to excuse themselves from collective worship. This legislation was brought into force in Wales in February 2009.

If a school feels that it is not appropriate for the daily act of collective worship to be wholly or mainly of a broadly Christian character for some or all, or for a group of pupils, then it can apply to its Local Authority Standing Advisory Council on Religious Education (SACRE) to request disapplication of the requirement. If the disapplication of the requirement is granted by the SACRE this is called a 'determination' and it lasts for five years.

In one secondary school in Wales with a large proportion of Muslim and Sikh pupils, a determination was granted to provide opportunity for some students to attend a Muslim act of worship and for others to attend one for Sikhs for part of the week.

Guidance documents produced by WASACRE (June 2012) and Estyn (September 2013) are available to provide further guidance on collective worship.

(M) WOMEN IN MUSLIM SOCIETY

46. What is the position of women in Muslim society?

It is inconceivable in Islam that any devout Muslim would treat women as inferior beings on the basis of religion. Muhammad (PBUH) was a champion for gender equality and fairness for women. He not only prohibited but actively prevented men's ill-treatment and oppression of women. He established the woman's right to own property as well as her right to inheritance. He defended her right of choosing or refusing a man for marriage*, as well as initiating divorce in cases of ill treatment or oppression. However, within the context of a mutually respectful marriage a Muslim woman would normally be expected to defer to her husband (Noble Qur'an. Surah 4:34). However, if he asks her to commit a forbidden action, which includes anything harmful, demeaning to her dignity, or in contravention of either her own or another's rights, she would be expected to refuse. Prophet Muhammad (PBUH) says there is no obedience to a created being in anything that entails disobedience of Allah.

In western democracy all have equal rights and schools must avoid discrimination on the grounds of gender, faith or race.

*Note that Islam prohibits that parents force their daughters or sons into a marriage they don't want. (See point 43)

47. Should a male member of staff try to shake hands with a Muslim female?

No. At best it will embarrass the female. At worst it is disrespectful as the female has been brought up to avoid physical contact with all males except those in her family. This advice applies when dealing with both students and parents. Similarly Muslim male parents are unlikely to shake a female member of staff's hand. Teachers will understand this is not disrespectful, but a sign of their respect for the standing of the female.

N.B This applies 'equally' to Muslim men and women. It is not more forbidden for women than men. Note that some Muslims may not follow this tradition.

48. Should a member of staff give additional tuition or carry out a detention with one student on his or her own?

No. This advice applies when dealing with any pupil of any background. Potentially the member of staff leaves himself/herself open to accusation. The school is likely to have a clear policy on this. Islam would demand that a boy/girl student should not be 'enclosed' with a teacher of the opposite sex in any circumstances.

(N) APPLYING SCHOOL DISCIPLINE

49. What do you do if two Muslim girls are fighting in the playground?

The school should have a policy, as does the Welsh Government (WG), on when it is right and proper for a member of staff to intervene. WG's policy allows a teacher to intervene when pupils are in danger of hurting themselves or others. The action a teacher chooses to take will be the same as for all students – except that a male teacher or a male student (Muslim or non-Muslim) should not lay their hands on a girl, unless there is no other alternative. If you can quickly establish with other Muslim students the necessity to intervene they can witness your intervention, if you decide it is imperative that you go ahead. In this case, the teacher must declare his intentions and call for appropriate backup from another member of staff. On each occasion, report the incident immediately and ensure that senior management takes witness statements. The school will wish to follow its normal procedures. All staff are advised to follow school policy and ensure that they are members of an association/union. A school policy should protect both the interests of the child and the member of staff acting reasonably and within school policy and the law.

50. Can a Muslim boy refuse to obey a female teacher/ teacher's aide?

No. By sending a pupil to school parents accept the discipline of the school. In cases of discipline the school's normal procedures should be used. Islam teaches the young to respect and learn from others. Note: there is no injunction in Islam that forbids men from obeying women. In fact, respect for authority is required as part of maintaining social cohesion. One cannot choose.

51. Can Muslim students be kept in detention, particularly at times of prayer?

Yes. It is lawful to keep pupils in detention after the school day. The school will have a policy on detention. It will also be mindful of all pupil and family needs and may make alternative arrangements, in special circumstances. It may be that a room for prayer is made available to the student before his/her detention starts. This will take no more than five or ten minutes.

52. What do I do if there is tension between pupils from two Muslim communities, which represent different sects of Muslims?

A strong lead from the head teacher, senior management team and governors is required. A sensible school will quickly engage with local community leaders, police and community workers in such situations and ensure that there is a regular and on-going dialogue. The school will already have policy and practice which require respect amongst the student body for each other. It will also have a range of sanctions under its disciplinary procedures which can be used for transgressors.

Note: In any case, Islam prohibits such fighting and arguments.

(0) BUILDING CONTACT AND TRUST WITH PARENTS AND THE COMMUNITY

53. How can I build a relationship with parents?

This is something that most schools are good at. There may be the need to build a relationship with parents who have moved into the district or with communities that find the school a daunting place. The school will be aware of this and should employ relevant strategies to build trust. Schools have used some, or all, of the following strategies:

- ensure school staff are welcoming (in person/email/by telephone/through the school website/intranet)
- using staff from the school who are representative of that community to make personal contact
- through the use of individuals who speak the relevant language or dialect
- by hiring an individual to work with pupils from a given community
- by running a parents' evening for a small number of new parents during the school day, so that they can see their children at work and by providing a cup of tea/coffee e.g. with asylum seekers
- by providing free transport for all parents from a particular district to come up to a parents' evening at school
- by holding a parents' evening in the locality in a community hall near to homes
- by setting up a particular community parents' group, which meets with a senior member of staff monthly to plan strategies and evaluate success
- by publishing the annual report in community languages
- by teaching relevant community languages
- by using pupil role models from that community and publicising success stories
- by displaying photographs of successful students (with permission) in school corridors

- by reporting student success through the school newspaper/ broadsheet
- by having a positive and regular school media profile (with parental permission)
- by establishing points of contact with local faith leaders
- by being aware of – and sensitive to – the various cultural and religious differences and needs within the community
- by encouraging representatives from ethnic groups to apply for the governing body
- through the daily work of the school demonstrating that ALL pupils are equally valued.

54. If I need to, what is the best way to make direct contact with the home?

Although schools traditionally write to parents it should be remembered that some parents from ethnic backgrounds will not be able to read and/or fully understand the school's message. For this reason, it is preferable to use somebody they already know. Very often it is left up to the mother to have contact with the school. It is therefore better if a female visits the home. An education welfare officer or a school community worker are often ideal people, particularly if they have community language skills.

55. Can I use a pupil to translate where a parent does not understand English?

You may if there is no other community language speaker available. But be aware as a pupil's translation can vary widely from what you are saying/asking! Also bear in mind that second generations of children may not have the language skills to translate adequately, and be embarrassed about this.

56. Is it worth making contact with the local mosque?

The RE/Philosophy and Beliefs/Ethics department may have already made contact and be taking groups there. If so you can build upon this as a school. The Imam may well be a useful source of knowledge and his wisdom/advice may well be worth listening to. It is advisable to make contact with the mosque rather than expecting them to make contact with you. Often it takes time to build relationships and trust, but stress that together you can do an even better job for Muslim students and society at large. It is important that the head teacher and governors give a lead in promoting and supporting community links.

(P) PRAYER WITHIN SCHOOL

57. Should I provide a prayer room for Muslim students at lunch times?

You may get requests from students and/or parents for this facility – and indeed, you may decide to ask suitable senior students or parents to facilitate.

Parents – and all outside facilitators – would need to be DBS (police) checked. If you decide not to allow lunch time prayers you should take advice from your Local Authority and explore any possible legal implications. (N.B. see legal obligation in point 59 below)

Note: Institutions may receive requests for access to a prayer room from Muslim teachers. This will assist with running the facility.

58. What happens if Muslim girls request a prayer room?

If you have provided one for the boys then you would need to do the same for girls as they have an equal right to pray. The law allows for single sex prayers to be held. Be aware that during the holy month of Ramadan numbers wishing to pray are likely to increase.

59. Are these prayer rooms off-limits to staff?

Certainly not. Indeed, recent legislation, in force from 1st July 2015, places an obligation on all schools and colleges to ensure that this facility is properly regulated, 'ensuring that any visiting speakers – whether invited by staff or students themselves – are suitable and appropriately supervised.' (paragraph 68 'Revised Prevent Duty Guidance: for England and Wales.' July 2015) Ensuring oversight for the management of such a facility would also involve e.g. compliance with health and safety requirements. Pupils need to know the times the prayer facility is open and the rules governing its use, so that they can abide by them. Experience has often shown that this activity is important to pupils and that – with clear guidance and supervision – it runs without incident.

60. What facilities are required for lunchtime prayer and how long does the lunchtime prayer take?

Muslims perform a ritual of washing before prayer which is called wudu. Pupils will need a facility to wash and cleanse themselves – hands up to the elbow, mouth, nose, face, as well as the feet up to the ankles. A room near to changing facilities or toilet block is best. A wall tap in a shower area is particularly effective, or a low level elongated wash basin to accommodate hands and feet. (Sometimes there are complaints about the residual water left on floors in toilets after wudu. This isn't easy to avoid, so providing a mop can make all the difference and encourage the pupils to keep the floor as dry as possible). Pupils will require prayer mats or carpet strips. Storage should be thought out before choosing the room/hall. Prayer takes no more than 5 or 10 minutes. Schools operating a prayer room should fix the times for prayer taking into consideration the effects of the lunar calendar and the practical measures of providing school dinners/sandwiches for those pupils requiring them.

61. By providing a prayer room am I 'pandering' to Muslim students?

No. "Fairness not favours" is an appropriate response to this concern. Prayer room provision allows the diverse identity of students to be manifested in a public setting such as school, college or university, which fosters confidence and openness. Not catering for a student's perceived needs gives the impression they are not welcome or do not belong in that space. The same can be said of any student's needs – recognising student identity (be this e.g. religion, sexual orientation, race etc...) should not be optional.

Institutions will have their own mission statements and ethos, but in general terms a school/college may take the view that as long as an activity does not harm others and as long as it promotes the needs of its students it can be allowed. Schools/colleges may also take the view that students do not always need to do exactly the same thing as their peers and that in true unity there is diversity.

When students have learnt to demonstrate and appreciate this you may feel they are a good way to becoming 'good citizens'.

62. Do the prayer times vary throughout the year/calendar and if so how can I manage to run the timetable?

Prayer times do vary throughout the Muslim calendar. In practice it is usually not possible to alter the school/college day or to allow pupils to leave lessons to pray. At some periods the lunchtime prayer times will fall outside the lunch period e.g. in the summer term. However, schools can provide rooming facilities after the school day.

Note: As prayer times vary slightly across the UK, schools are advised to check with the local mosque. As general guidelines:
- In the winter time (October-March) pupils may pray any time from 12.00 – 2.00 p.m.
- In the summer time (April-September) pupils may pray from 1.30 – 4.00 p.m. which means that pupils do not have to pray in school.

However, there may be some who choose to do so.

See also the following link for UK-wide information concerning prayer times. www.islamicfinder.org.

63. What happens if I have a group of Muslim students on a field trip or educational visit?

There should be no difficulty. Pupils can pray, for example whilst on a biology/geography field trip, by placing their mats down on (e.g.) the beach/floor of a glaciated valley. Allowing for the ten minutes required should not prove difficult. Pupils should be given the responsibility of packing/unloading their prayer mats at the start/end of the day.

(Q) HOLOCAUST DAY

64. Many Local Authorities hold memorial services on this day and request readers from various local schools to highlight 'man's treatment of man'. If requested should I allow my pupils to attend?

Yes, providing there is no pressure applied and the pupil does so of his/her own free will. Parents should be informed.

(R) LAW

65. How should schools operate?

British schools must operate and stay within the law as set out by Parliament and devolved governments. They should be mindful also of guidance from these bodies and from various other quasi-government bodies.

66. What is sharia law?

Sharia (or 'fiqh', meaning jurisprudence) is a set of ethical and moral principles that govern personal and communal religious interaction amongst Muslims. It is diverse and dynamic. It is not codified, and varies from place to place and in fact even person to person. The majority of Sharia is in reference to religious observances, such as what to eat, how to pray, and certain ceremonies, such as marriage, and divorce, as well as principles relating to financial ethics. A very small aspect of Sharia law refers to punishments, or hudood. No religious scholar would advocate the application of punishment in the UK.

Because Sharia is not codified, it is open to debate, discussion and change by specialists/scholars. Sharia law is derived from the Quran and the Hadith, which are codified, but it is important to stress they are not the same thing.

In non-Muslim majority countries like the UK, Sharia law is not intended to challenge nation state law (i.e. one law for one people), and historically, has never been applied in such a way.

Many Muslim-majority countries describe their legal and penal system as Sharia. This is usually to give it religious legitimacy. The legal systems of Pakistan, Saudi Arabia and Iran (all countries which claim their legal systems are Sharia) vary widely from each other.

(3) HIGHER EDUCATIONAL INSTITUTIONS

(S) A RANGE OF RESPONSES TO EVERYDAY SCENARIOS

67. What's unique about the university context?

Universities contain young and idealistic students (sometimes from overseas) who are exploring their boundaries and identities as adults for the first time. Universities are also places which research new, and sometimes radical, concepts, all of which can lead to vulnerability.

68. Are there specific rules about what I can and can't do in university?

There is a large amount of law that directly relates to Universities (and staff).To deal with this most universities will have Prevent Coordinators who will work with the Equality & Diversity and Ethics committees which will all offer guidance. Students should be reassured that they can approach these members of staff for guidance and support. Much of the discourse surrounding Prevent at universities seems to focus on claimed restrictions on freedom of speech, and the perception that Prevent teams are 'policing' and monitoring students on the basis of racial and/or faith bias and assumptions. For some, these concerns have been heightened as a result of counter-terrorism legislation which came into effect as of 1st July for schools in England and Wales and 18th September 2015 for colleges and universities.

69. Whom should I approach if I have concerns about sexism, religious intolerance or lack of respect or if I am concerned that a student may be in the process of being radicalised?

Most universities now have a specific member of staff who operates as their 'Prevent Coordinator'. They will be trained to work with external agencies able to help as well as having strong community and faith links. Chaplains and Student Services staff are excellent sources for help and advice.

70. If a student asks to attend Eid celebrations overseas, will they be allowed to attend?

Universities are required by equality legislation to make reasonable adjustments for specific faith groups. Students should, however, always make their requests known before taking leave and such absence may not be able to be facilitated by the establishment.

71. A student wants to start an Islamic Society/Group, what should they do?

Most universities focus all of their student groups and societies through the Student Union and this should be the first point of contact. It should be noted that religious societies are almost universally positive and many students find them a useful source of strength and positive self-identity.

72. A Muslim student has just suffered bereavement, what support might I provide?

The death of a loved one is perhaps the hardest issue to face but especially in a university which can be a lonely place. Different Muslim traditions have different religious and cultural needs associated with death and these constitute an important part of the grieving process. Most UK universities have significant numbers of international students from Muslim countries who have a range of different faith-based and culturally sensitive bereavement and death practices. As well as the obvious bereavement/counselling sessions, the individual needs of the student have to be considered in light of their own cultural practice, and specialist advice might need to be sought in this context to ensure appropriate duty of care.

4. UNDERSTANDING ISLAM IN THE WORLD TODAY

(T) MUSLIM GROUPS

73. What are the major Muslim groups?

During the lifetime of the Prophet Muhammad (PBUH) all Muslims stood together as one group. After his death in 632 AD divisions arose due to (i) disputes regarding his successor and (ii) at a later date, differences regarding interpretation of the Qur'an and Hadith. Today there exist several groups of Muslims, with Sunni and Shia being the two major ones. Salafi, Deobandis and Barelvis are examples of sub-groups within the Sunni tradition. Sufi orders can be found in both the Sunni and Shia traditions. Sunni Muslims make up approximately 87%-90% of all Muslims across the world.

The most significant divisions within the Islamic juristic tradition are Sunni, Shia and Ibadi.

Within the Sunni tradition, there are many different expressions of Islam. These include reformist movements (such as the Salafiyyah or Salafis, from Saudi Arabia, or the Deobandi School, from South Asia) as well as what can be called 'traditional' Islam (those which follow the 'four schools' or 'madhabs'). Some of these advocate political activism whereas others are politically quietist. The lines between them are blurred, and a pupil may derive his or her understanding of Islam from a multiplicity of sources.

Shias or Shi'ites are found particularly in Iran and Iraq, where they are the majority. There are also significant minorities in Yemen, Lebanon, Syria, Bahrain and other places.

Shias can be from several various traditions, but the most common is called the Ithna Ashari.

Ibadi Muslims are a small group, mainly but not exclusively from Oman. The majority of Muslims in Oman are Ibadi. They are not well known even amongst Sunnis or Shias, and can sometimes be viewed with suspicion by other Muslims because of this.

All these groups noted above accept the same fundamental beliefs outlined in section 1 of this guide. It should be noted however, that differences between some of these groups (e.g. Sunnis and Shias) have resulted in on-going violence towards each other in some parts of the world, e.g. Iraq, Pakistan.

In some places around the world there are conflicts which run across sectarian differences. For example, in Syria, the Assad government is associated with a sect within Shi'a Islam while ISIS/ISIL/Daesh claims to be a predominantly Sunni movement. The latter group is rejected by the majority of Muslims as they are considered to be 'Khawarij', or those who have exited from a true understanding of Islam and advocated violence as a means of propagation. Although it would be wrong to categorise these conflicts as sectarian in nature, they do sometimes inflame tensions between religious groups.

It is not within the scope of this guide to give a more detailed classification and should you need, you are advised to seek out appropriate references to gain greater depth and understanding – taking a broad spectrum of sources.

(U) MUSLIM POPULATIONS

74. What are the figures?

With a total world population of seven billion, Muslims make up 1.6 billion, or 23% of the total. Only Christianity, of all the world's great religions, has more followers. Muslim majority countries stretch across North Africa to the horn of Africa and across the Red Sea to the Arabian Peninsula and the Middle East. There are also large Muslim populations in the Balkans (Albania, Bosnia, Kosovo), Russia and China. Western Europe also has a Muslim population, which in Britain's case numbers over three million out of a total population of about sixty five million, or 4.6%. In parts of Asia there are very significant Muslim populations – in Pakistan, Bangladesh, Indonesia and India. 60% of all Muslims live in Asia. There are 50 countries world-wide where there is a Muslim majority. The largest Muslim country by population is Indonesia with 12.9% of the world's Muslims. Pakistan has 11.1%; India 10.3% (although there is a Hindu majority); Bangladesh 9.3%; Egypt and Nigeria have 5% each; Iran and Turkey 4.7% each; Iraq and Saudi Arabia 2% each; Sudan 1.9%; Syria 1.3%; and Russia and Niger 1%.

Where Muslim populations are in the minority within a country, such as the United Kingdom or other countries in Western Europe, it is vital that their rights and responsibilities as citizens are respected and encouraged – as would be the case for all minority groups.

(V) CONFLICTS IN THE MIDDLE EAST

75. Why, as teachers and trainers do we need to know about a series of wars and conflicts in the Middle East and Palestine and in particular the Arab/Israeli conflict?

Teachers and trainers will be aware that conflicts that occur in foreign countries – for whatever reason – can re-ignite in classrooms, playgrounds and work-based learning environments here in Great Britain. Advance knowledge and understanding of key issues between pupils with opposing views can assist in preventing and/or resolving tensions and hostility.

The Middle East covers the area of the Arabian Peninsula (Saudi Arabia, Yemen, Oman, United Arab Emirates, Bahrain, Kuwait), and the territories of the following states – Egypt, Israel, Jordan, Palestine (not fully recognised as a sovereign state world-wide at this point in time), Lebanon, Syria, Iraq, Iran, Turkey.

Muslims often see the foreign policies of the Western Powers (e.g. the USA, the UK) as protecting their oil interests in the region, and believe this is not helpful to establishing a set of peaceful solutions to very complex situations.

Teachers of history will be aware of the precise details of the Arab/Israeli conflict centred on the biblical lands of Palestine, for it is sometimes a part of syllabi and examination courses.

Any solution involves the lives of Israelis and Palestinians and the deep distrust within many sections of those communities. Israel was set up in 1948 by the United Nations as a home for the Jewish people, who had suffered terribly under the Nazis. Some six million Jews had been exterminated. The Jews had not had a national home for two millennia.

Before the First World War Palestine and most of the Arabian Peninsula was part of the Ottoman Empire, centred on Turkey. During this war Bedouin tribes, with Lawrence of Arabia, fought a guerilla war behind enemy lines; perhaps their most famous exploit was the taking of the town of Aqaba. After the war some Arab states were set up, but the League of Nations gave the French the mandate to rule Syria and the British authority over Palestine.

After the Second World War the British announced their withdrawal from Palestine and the United Nations drew up its partition plan, giving land to a Jewish state. Palestinians living in those areas would either have to move or remain as Muslim citizens in a Jewish state. The state of Israel was set up with the help of the USA in 1948. The first of four wars over the next quarter of a century was fought and Israel was successful in establishing its borders. A large number of Palestinians fled their lands fearing the worst. A sizeable refugee problem was created, which neither the Israelis or Arabs, or the UN, have resolved to this day.

In 1956 war broke out between Egypt on the one side and Britain, France and Israel on the other. It was over the control of the Suez Canal. In the 1967 war Israel took the Golan Heights from Syria, the West Bank from Jordan, and Gaza from Egypt. In the 1973 war, sometimes called the Yom Kippur war (because it started on the holiest day in the Jewish calendar), Israel clung on to its gains, but subsequently made peace with Egypt and Jordan. Gaza became a Palestinian encampment and with The West Bank was seen by Palestinians as their homeland. They wanted the establishment of a Palestinian state.

World powers have been unable to get the protagonists to agree peace. Each war has brought more refugees, some of whom have resorted/retaliated to violence with the state of Israel. Israel has continued to build settlements on the West Bank lands of the Palestinians.

The Palestinians, for their part, have split into two main factions, one in Gaza and one on the West Bank, each with its own agenda. Palestine remains an issue for Muslims and for the World.

For Muslims the solution to the Arab/Israeli conflict remains a high priority and the West's perceived involvement – and the perception by some that they have not been 'honest brokers' – in the conflict has caused much resentment.

76. How have the Gulf Wars affected Muslim opinion?

There have been two Gulf Wars between Iraq and the West. The first lasted from 1990-1 and occurred when the then Iraqi leader, Saddam Hussein, invaded his neighbour Kuwait. A UN force led by the USA drove the Iraqi army out of Kuwait and back towards Baghdad. It is generally accepted that Saddam Hussein was a cruel despot, ruling his country with a rod of iron and taking revenge on any Iraqi who stood in his way. However, many Muslims have difficulty with what they see as the West's interference in the Muslim world and believe it is motivated by their desire to protect oil supplies. The second Gulf War was backed by a UN Security Council resolution requiring the leader of Iraq, Saddam Hussein, to end his nuclear, biological and chemical programmes. He had used chemical weapons against the Kurds in northern Iraq and cruelly put down the Marsh Arabs in the south – all Iraqi citizens. Both the USA's President and the British Prime Minister claimed that Saddam Hussein had weapons of mass destruction ('WMDs') and that he failed to satisfy international demands. An American and British-led force invaded Iraq in 2003. Most Muslim opinion was against the actions of President George W. Bush and Prime Minister Tony Blair and many British non-Muslim citizens also strongly objected to the actions on the grounds that there was no UN resolution for the invasion of Iraq.

Whilst Saddam Hussein was removed from power it is generally accepted that the Americans and British had not thought out a sufficient post-war reconstruction plan. Religious strife between

Sunni and Shia broke out in the vacuum that followed and foreign troops became hated and targeted. It took Britain until 2010 and the USA until 2011 to extricate themselves from Iraq. Post-invasion it has been shown beyond reasonable doubt that the original reasons for the invasion (i.e. that Iraq had weapons of mass destruction) were unfounded.

77. What are the brief facts about the Iran-Iraq War of 1980-88?

In 1979 the pro-Western Shah of Iran was toppled from power by Islamic revolutionaries. The new leader was a hard-line cleric named Ruholah Khomeini. The country remains under the rule of his successors. There was much anti-Western feeling, which focused on anti- American activities. In 1980 the forces of Iraq, under Saddam Hussein, invaded Iran, following a number of border disputes. Iran is an oil producer and exporter. Iraq sought to replace Iran as the regional power. Some Muslims felt that Iraq was unjustly given tacit support by the West in order to remove Khomeini. Some British schools had both Iraqi and Iranian children on their rolls and they wisely gained the support of both their local Iraqi and Iranian communities to ensure that foreign conflict was not brought into school and local communities.

(W) THE BALKANS WAR

78. How did the Balkan War affect the peoples of the former Yugoslavia?

The breakup of modern-day Yugoslavia and the establishment of several nation states led to the Balkan War of 1991-5. In simple terms it was a war between Serbia on the one side and Croats and Bosnians on the other. There was also war between the Bosniaks (Muslim Bosnians) and the Croats and between the various factions within Bosnia.

The Bosnian War of 1992-5 saw some of the worst excesses since the Second World War, with concentration camps and massacres of young boys and men. Multi-ethnic Bosnia was made up of Bosniak Muslims (44%), Orthodox Christian Serbs (31%) and Catholic Croats (17%). All sides were involved in war crimes, but the worst and majority of the acts were carried out against the Bosniaks. The UN became involved, but failed to protect Srebrenica, a Bosniak safehaven, where 8000 Muslims were slaughtered. The UN declared Srebrenica a protected safe zone, to which many Bosniak civilian refugees fled to avoid the fighting. When the Serbians approached the protected safe zone, the UN peacekeeping force failed to act and instead allowed the Serbian forces to take the area and carry out a genocide which saw over 8000 killed.

The perpetrators have subsequently been taken to the War Crimes Court in The Hague. American and British action against Serbia ended the war. Muslims point to the failure of the international community in not stopping the genocide.

(X) 9/11, 7/7 and AFGHANISTAN

79. How are 9/11 and 7/7 linked to Afghanistan and to measures introduced by Western governments?

The September 11th 2001 terrorist attacks on the Twin Towers of New York's World Trade Centre and on the Pentagon, and the London bus and tube bombings of July 7th 2005 (as well as those in other European capitals) brought an absolute commitment by the Western powers to track down and deal with terrorists both at home and abroad. It also affected defence policy by leaders taking actions in several parts of the world.

The destruction of the Twin Towers, by al-Qa'ida, and the loss of 3000 innocent lives led directly to USA's intervention in Afghanistan in 2001. The Taliban regime, which harboured al-Qa'ida and its leader Osama bin Laden, were driven from power by the joint forces of the United Afghan Front, the USA and Britain and other countries. An interim government under Hamid Karzai was established. Whilst bin Laden was finally tracked down to a northern Pakistani town in 2011 and killed, the Taliban have been resurgent from their Pakistani bases. Their successful campaign of planting explosive devices on roads and in fields and their use of suicide bombers has resulted in the deaths of over four thousand Allied troops and ten thousand Afghani nationals. The history of Afghanistan shows that foreign troops are resented by much of the population and that in the end they have to leave. 2014 has seen the withdrawal of western troops and the election of a new president for Afghanistan.

(Y) THE ARAB SPRING – 2011

80. How will the Arab Spring affect the relationship between the Muslim World and the West?

The term 'Arab Spring' refers to the demands of citizens to have a say in the running of their country. It began in Tunisia where civil protest brought about the overthrow of a dictatorship. It moved on to Egypt with the same result. The successful fight by Libyans against their dictator, Colonel Gaddafi, was also part of this popular uprising. The question for the West and for Muslims in general was how to stop the killing by Gaddafi of his people, without putting ground forces into Libya. The West appears to have learnt from its failures in Iraq and in Bosnia, by providing aerial support to stop the killing and by accepting that only Libyans can decide their future. Intervention into Libya was also hotly disputed amongst Muslims. Some considered it valuable; others considered it to be problematic in the same way as Iraq was. It was hoped that this policy would help build relationships between the Muslim World and the West. However, when a dictator is removed instability often results and it is left to a course of events within the country to decide its future path. A number of factions vie for control. The burning of the American Embassy in Benghazi, Libya, and the murder of the Ambassador by extremists is an example of this. The whole region remains unstable at the present time and time will tell if the democratic demands of citizens portrayed in the Arab Spring will be realised – and if so, to what extent.

Popular uprisings have been put down by force in Bahrain and excessive force continues to be used against Syrians by their Government. A Civil War is raging. The UN has been unsuccessful in stopping it and hundreds of thousands of Syrians have fled to refugee camps in neighbouring states. In the latter months of 2015, the world witnessed a modern day exodus of humanity from the region across Europe, with little apparent agreement or strategy on the part of European leaders to deal with a growing humanitarian crisis. One glimmer of hope at the end of 2016 came in the form of a resolution from the UN Security Council which has unanimously endorsed efforts by Russia and Turkey to end the nearly six year conflict in Syria and jump-start peace negotiations. Moscow is reported as saying that it hopes to bring Donald Trump's administration on board.

One of the groups fighting against the Syrian government is ISIL (the Islamic State of Iraq and the Levant), a Sunni terrorist group which originated in 1999 and grew in strength with the Western invasion of Iraq in 2003. It used the vacuum created by the civil war and the lack of agreement by the great powers of what action should be taken. It is also known as ISIS (the Islamic State of Iraq and Syria) or simply IS. (See following chapter 'Demystifying ISIS/ IS') It has proclaimed a worldwide Caliphate, claiming religious authority over all Muslims. However, the group does not represent any of the main Sunni schools of Islam nor are their leaders versed in Islamic jurisprudence. It is widely known for its abuse of civil rights, which has included beheadings and ethnic cleansing against the Sunnis, Shias, Kurds, Christians, other religious sects, Iraqi troops and Westerners. The biggest victims of IS attacks have been ordinary Iraqi and Syrian Muslims who do not adhere to their ideology and doctrine. Muslims have also been the primary opponents who have fought IS and hampered its growth.

The group has a very well-developed propaganda machine, and uses the internet to proclaim and spread its message and to draw in fighters from Western and other Muslim communities. It is claimed that over 800 young British Muslims have left to join ISIS by the end of 2016, thus causing distress within the British Muslim community and within British society.

The issue of returning jihadist fighters from areas of conflict is an increasing concern, with the UK government determining its response on a case-by-case basis.

Atrocities committed in its name – for example, 'Charlie Hebdo' in January 2015; the Bataclan atrocity in November 2015, both in Paris – allied to so-called 'lone wolf' attacks such as in Nice in July 2016 and Berlin in December 2016 have brought international (UN) condemnation.

(Z) AFRICA

81. Where is Mali and what is going on?

Mali is a large country in West Africa with a population of some 14-15 million. Its capital is Bamako, which lies in the south of the country. Much of the north reaches into the Sahara desert. In January 2012 armed Tuareg tribesmen took control of much of the north, dissatisfied with their treatment by the southern government. The Tuareg are a nomadic people found in much of the middle and western Sahara (Mali, Niger, southern Algeria and Libya and smaller numbers in north Nigeria and Burkina Faso). They have camel and cattle herds and have dominated the caravan trade across the Sahara. They cross borders regularly in search of grazing and water. Subsequently, Islamist extremists (Ansar Dine) took over control of the uprising and by December were threatening the south. In response to requests from the Malian government French troops, with Malian forces, were deployed to drive back the rebels and by late January 2013 they had reached the northern town of Timbuktu. At the same time the African Union met in Ethiopia, many of the countries promising to send troops of their own to support the Malian government. The extremists, for now, have vanished into the desert. Mali and adjacent countries, together with the West, fear the increase in strength of extremist Islamic factions and the activities they engage in, such as the recent attack on an oil and gas installation in southern Algeria, which cost many lives and brought further instability to the region. Answers to the problems in Mali lie in a political solution being found between the Malian Government and the Tuareg peoples and with the use of African Union and Malian troops to police the country. France's initial involvement has been welcomed by the town dwellers in the central and northern districts, but increasingly there is a growing belief amongst international observers that the solution to the violence and instability is likely to be long and drawn out – as evidenced by the declaration of a state of emergency after the bloody nine-hour hostage-taking at the Radisson Blu hotel in the capital Bamako on 20th November 2015, exactly a week after the Paris massacre.

82. Where is Nigeria and what is going on?

Nigeria is a huge West African country with a large Christian population in the south and a Muslim population in the north. Boko Haram is a militant Sunni Islamist group based in north-east Nigeria, and is responsible for killing more than 5 million civilians in the five-year period up to 2014. Nigerian politicians and the military have proved ineffective in countering Boko Haram, which forbids non-Muslim education and pronounces any Western influence as a sin. In April 2014 they kidnapped 276 schoolgirls from Chibok in northern Nigeria, reportedly to use as 'negotiating pawns'. In October 2016, 21 of the remaining students in captivity were freed. The Nigerian government said their release was the result of negotiations with Swiss officials acting as intermediaries with Boko Haram. Nigeria's Information Minister Lai Mohammed said that their release was "the first step" towards the liberation of all the remaining girls.

Boko Haram had initially pledged bayat (allegiance) to Al Qaeda and has reportedly switched this pledge to endorse ISIS/ISIL/Daesh, with internal disagreements on this move reported.

83. Where are Somalia and Kenya and what is going on?

Somalia lies in the Horn of Africa, has suffered years of civil war, and now with the aid of African Union troops and US military support, it has succeeded in reducing the influence of the Salafist terrorist jihadist organisation known as al-Shabaab. Al-Shabaab has replied by committing atrocities across the border of neighbouring Kenya (whose troops are part of the African Union force), which have included the terrorist attack on the Nairobi shopping complex, resulting in the deaths of 67 people. Al-Shabaab have also engaged in kidnappings and murders of Western tourists on Kenya's Indian Ocean coast. The group continues to carry out attacks in Somalia itself, e.g. attacking the Presidential compound, Villa Somalia, in Mogadishu.

Perhaps the example of two Cardiff teenagers, who were successfully returned home from the Kenyan border when they tried to cross into Somalia to train with al-Shabaab in October 2011, shows that where the parents, the local Muslim community, the police, security services and the local MP work together, a successful conclusion can be reached.

5. DEMYSTIFYING ISIS/IS

84. ISIS claims that its actions are founded in Islamic teachings. Is this true?

The group's Arabic name is Al-Dawla al-Islamiya fi al-Iraq wa al-Sham which forms the acronym Daesh. Daesh can also be understood as a play on words and an insult. Depending on the context of how it is understood in Arabic, Daesh can mean:

★ "To trample down and crush"

★ "A bigot who imposes his view on others" (plural use)

The group does not endorse the name as it does not spell out the crucial Islamic component and has threatened to cut out the tongues of anyone who uses the term Daesh. Countries in the Middle East as well as France and Australia use the term Daesh as opposed to ISIL, ISIS or IS. Increasingly, the term is used in the UK.

Although Daesh is widely known for its visualisation of terrorism by filming and murdering its victims on camera, which is then uploaded on the internet, lesser known is that the biggest number of victims of Daesh attacks have been ordinary Iraqi and Syrian Muslims who do not adhere to their ideology and doctrine.

Some of the actions against Muslims by Daesh include executing university professors, journalists and clerics who have refused to endorse beheadings. Daesh have also thrown people from the top of buildings for allegedly being homosexual, raising birds in their garden and watching football on television. They have also executed married couples for putting decorations on their car. All these people murdered were Muslims. This includes women and children whose Islamic faith is very important and who do not get involved in politics.

The text that Daesh uses to justify their violence against ordinary Muslims is 'The Management of Savagery: The Most Critical Stage Through Which the Umma Will Pass' by an individual known as Abu Bakr Naji. Naji's real identity remains unknown which on its own should undermine Daesh's ideological justification.

Published on the Internet in 2004, 'The Management of Savagery' uses religion as a tool for legitimisation as opposed to tailoring itself to an adherence of Islamic jurisprudence. There are virtually no citations from the Qur'an, Hadith and Sunnah.

Savagery is a conceptual doctrine which enables operations to be conducted with unity of purpose without constant communication. Similar to the German doctrine of Auftragstakti, the development of mission-type tactics has enabled Daesh commanders to give cadres general directions of what needs to be achieved, allowing them the freedom to determine how to carry out these directions.

Rather than presenting an ideology that is based on Islamic theology, 'Management of Savagery' reinvents history and tradition whilst trying to create an illusion of power. The irony, is that the very treatise that Daesh uses for religious justification, does not refer to the central tenets of Islam.

Savagery is at the core of Daesh's ideology and 'Management of Savagery' justifies beheadings of Muslims and non-Muslims as not only permissible but recommended. Yet, this is sanctioned without any religious citations and therefore illustrates that if Daesh cannot base their violent justifications in religious texts, then they will fabricate it to justify their own ends.

(6) UNDERSTANDING AND DETECTING VULNERABITY – A PROFESSIONAL PERSPECTIVE

85. Over the years, much has been written about 'vulnerability' in the popular press and checklists of possible signs to watch out for have been published with alarming recklessness – from turned up trousers to long beards to face coverings. This approach has done little to support the student or enhance the understanding and knowledge of the teacher/lecturer whose key function is to support and offer help and guidance.

It is understood that this section cannot do other than 'light touch' this important area – but crucially, from the perspective of a practising consultant psychiatrist.

Vulnerability can be understood as the diminished capacity of an individual or group to anticipate, cope with, resist and recover from the impact of a particular stress. The concept is relative and dynamic; vulnerability is associated with a number of factors, such as social group, gender, age and so forth. Often, vulnerable people are isolated, insecure and defenseless in the face of the challenge they face.

The opposite of vulnerability is capacity or resilience, which is equally defined as the ability of an individual or group to cope with or resist a particular challenge. Things that strengthen their resilience are often known as 'resources,' which may be financial, social, educational or others.

Given this, it becomes critical to understand two things: what stresses are a group vulnerable to, and what makes them vulnerable to them? From this, one can determine what kinds of resources are required to increase their resilience. In a sense, diagnosis and formulation precedes therapeutic engagement.

Why are Muslim youth vulnerable in this way? Some factors relate to themselves, some to their families and communities, some to the nature of the threat, and some to the more general environment. Some of these can be tackled directly by teachers and educators, others more indirectly.

It has been recognised for some time that ethnic minorities are more vulnerable generally, due to feelings of isolation, language and integration problems, or discrimination (real or perceived). A pervading sense of alienation from wider society, coupled with a feeling of disempowerment, is a major 'push' factor towards an Islamic extremism that appears to offer, on the face of it, both belonging and empowerment. Extremists are well aware of this, and will often play directly on such feelings – their advances have even been termed 'grooming of young Muslims' by some commentators, and the parallels are easy to spot.

Children of first generation immigrants also feel a sense of cultural, intellectual and even linguistic dislocation from their wider families and traditional understandings of Islam as represented by local Imams, who often have not grown up in the UK, don't speak English well, and are ill-equipped to deal with the challenges of being a young person in the UK. This makes them more vulnerable to attractively packaged, English-language promises of 'true Islam' rather than the 'cultural interpretations' of the local priest.

Are there any outward indicators of extremism? It is unlikely that those most afflicted by extremism will manifest any signs of it, as has been repeatedly seen in the unfortunate cases of those farthest gone. Those in earlier stages, however, may very well demonstrate their vulnerability in their attitudes and responses to world events, often on social media.

It should be borne in mind that increased outward religiosity (wearing a veil, growing a beard, praying more) are normal indicators of a deepening commitment to God and have no necessary link to extremism. Indeed, erroneous assumptions about this can contribute to – or even create – feelings of alienation that were not there to start with!

The explosion of the internet and social media usage plays a major role in enabling unfettered access to – and interaction with – extremist ideology. How to deal with this remains an open question; it is virtually impossible – given the realities of such communities – for parents to police their children's online activity. The way forward can only be providing a strong counter-narrative and allowing a safe space for young people to discuss their feelings, beliefs and opinions. Plugging the spout only damages the kettle.

In the context of this present work, if Muslim youth are perceived as being vulnerable to a cruelly distorted – but compelling – image of Islam, the greatest resource to shore up their resilience is an equally compelling – but accurate – reflection. A sympathetic and trusted educator, no matter what their background, providing well-informed and authentic knowledge about the reality of Islam is a powerful antidote to the siren call of extremism. It is our hope (and prayer) that this work will be an important part of that resilience building.

(7) GLOSSARY

Al-Dawla al-Islamiya fi al-Iraq wa al-Sham	Arabic for Islamic State in Iraq and Syria
Allah	Arabic word for God
Al-Qa'ida	Meaning 'The Base", a global militant Sunni Islamist organization founded by Osama bin Laden. It operates as a network comprising both a multinational, stateless army and an Islamist, extremist group
Azaan *(also adhan)*	The call to prayer performed by the Mu'azzin *(also muezzin)*
Barelvis	A movement that originated in Bareilly in South Asia that follows the Sunni Hanafi school of jurisprudence. Followers prefer to be referred to as Ahle Sunnat wal Jama' meaning 'People of the traditions [of Muhammad] and the community' The largest communities of Muslims in Britain are from areas of Punjab and Kashmir where the Barelvi charismatic Sufi traditions are strongest.
Bayat	An oath of allegiance given to a Muslim ruler
Boko Haram	A militant Islamic group in Northern Nigeria who want to create a "pure" Islamic state ruled by sharia law. It has come to mean "Western education is forbidden"
Burka	A loose outer garment worn by some Muslim women to cover them from head to toe
Caliphate	The rule or reign or a Muslim ruler (Caliph)
Da'esh	"To trample down and crush" "A bigot who imposes his view on others" (plural use)

Deobandis	A Revivalist movement within Sunni Islam centered in South Asia and has recently spread to the United Kingdom with a presence in South Africa. The name comes from Deoband, India, where the school Darul Uloom Deoband is situated.
Dhikr *(also Zikr)*	Meaning remembrance of God by repeated recitation of phrases or prayers
Du'aa' *(also dua)*	An act of invocation, prayer or supplication
Eid	Festival / feast – used mainly in context of Eid ul Fitr (festival celebrating the end of Ramadan) and Eid ul Adha, Festival of Sacrifice. Also used by some for Eid Milad un Nabi (festival to celebrate the birth of Prophet Muhammad)
Five Pillars of Islam	Five articles of worship belief (shahadah), prayer (salah), fasting (sawm), (alms) zakat, pilgrimage (hajj)
Fiqh	Islamic jurisprudence that deals with the observance of rituals, morals and social legislation in Islam.
Fiqh al Sunnah	Islamic jurisprudence as explained according to Prophetic traditions
Four schools of thought or 'madhabs'	The four main doctrines followed by the majority of Sunni Muslims namely Hanafi, Maliki, Shafi and Hanbali
GOT (Getting On Together) Project	A series of counter-extremism programmes delivered to schools, colleges and youth and community sectors across England and Wales. Funded by the UK and Welsh Governments, the GOT 2 'Challenging Extremism' module has been adapted for the Welsh Baccalaureate and accredited by the WJEC Examination Board for use at KS4. A differentiated module has been accredited by Agored Cymru for use with Third Sector Organisations. The GOT Project is referenced on the DfE website 'Educate against hate' @educateagainsthate.com

Hadith	A collection of reports based on the sayings and actions of the Prophet Muhammad. The hadith are regarded as an important tool in understanding and commentating on the Quran
Hajj	One of the Five Pillars of Islam, hajj is the traditional pilgrimage made by Muslims to Mecca. The hajj takes place in the 12th month of the Islamic calendar, the month of Dhul Hijjah
Haram	Arabic term meaning something that is forbidden or sinful
Hudood	Islamic laws stating the limits ordained by God and including the deterrent punishments for serious crimes
Ibadi	A denomination in Islam that came out of the Kharijite movement. They have consistently opposed terrorist activity for over thirteen hundred years.
Ihsan	An Arabic term meaning excellence in the sight of and for God
Ijazah	Literal meaning perfection. Used to indicate that an individual has been authorised by a higher authority to transmit a certain Islamic knowledge
Imam	Muslim religious leader who is often the prayer leader in the mosque.
Injeel *(also Injil)*	Arabic term for the Gospel of Jesus Christ, one of the four divine books
Ismaili	Shia Imami Ismaili Muslims who belong to the Shia branch of Islam and generally referred known as the Ismailis
Ithna Ashari	Arabic for Twelvers (see Twelvers)
Jihad	The act of striving, applying oneself, struggling, persevering. Although this term is controversial Jihad is often incorrectly translated as "Holy War"

Ka'bah	A building at the center of Islam's most sacred mosque in mecca and considered the "House of God" on earth. The point towards which all Muslims pray.
Khawarij	Meaning literally 'those who went out'. Members of a sect that appeared in the first century of Islam and deviated from mainstream Islam. It was known for killing Muslims under allegations of excommunication *takfir*
Khutba	The Friday sermon given by the Imam before the congregational prayer
Madrassa	The Arabic word for any type of secular or religious educational institution
Makkah	Mecca
Mihrab	The niche in the wall of a mosque, at the point nearest to Mecca, toward which the congregation faces to pray
Mosque *(also Masjid)*	A place of worship for Muslims
Mu'azzin *(also muezzin)*	The official in the mosque who summons the congregation to pray by calling of the azaan *(also adhan)* from the minaret
Muharram	The first month of the Islamic calendar. The 10th day of the month is also referred to as 'Ashura' meaning Day of Remembrance. Ashura marks the climax of the Remembrance of Muharram and commemorates the death of Husayn ibn Ali, the grandson of Muhammad at the Battle of Karbala on 10 Muharram in the year 61 AH (680 CE)
Niqab	A traditional face veil worn by some Muslim women covering all but the eyes
PBUH	Meaning Peace Be Upon Him recited after the Prophet Muhammad's name as a sign of respect

Quran	The final message from God, enshrined in the Quran, one of the four divine books
Sahabah	Sahabah were the companions, disciples, scribes and family of the Prophet Muhammad
Salafi/ salafis/ salafiyyah	Ultra conservative doctrine within Sunni Islam that emulating the Prophet Muhammad and his earliest followers—al salaf al-salih, the 'pious predecessors'
Salah *(also salat)*	One of Five Pillars of Islam, performing of five daily prayers
SAW	Abbreviation for sallal-la-hu-alaihi-wa-salaam meaning Peace Be upon Him *(see PBUH)*
Sawm	Meaning fasting which is one of the five pillars of Islam, during the Holy month of Ramadan
Seveners	A branch of Ismaili Shias who belief that the seventh Imam Ismā'īl ibn Ja'far was the last Imām (hereditary leader of the Muslim community)
Shahadah	The declaration of faith and one of the five pillars of Islam
Shalwar Kamese *(also kameez)*	Traditional dress of men and women from Pakistan consisting of long tunic and baggy trousers
Sharia/ Shariah	A religious code for living in accordance with the Quran and the Sunnah
Sheikh/ Shaykh	A title used to refer to the male chief or head of an Arab tribe or family. More commonly used as a term of respect for community leaders. Female equivalent Sheikha / Shaykha
Shia / Shias / Shi'ites	An abbreviation for Shī'atu 'Alī meaning 'followers of Ali. Shias form 10-13% of the world Muslim population and believe the rightful successor after the Prophet Muhammad was his cousin and Son in law, Ali.

Sufi	Followers of Sufism often referred to as the mystical or spiritual dimension of Islam
Sunnah	Refers to the traditions and practices of the Prophet Muhammad
Sunni	Sunni Muslims form approximately 87%-90% of the world Muslim population. Sunni Muslims believe that the first Caliph after the death of the Prophet Muhammad was his father in law Abu Bakr.
Surah	A chapter of the Quran of which there are 114
Torah	One of the four divine books the torah is the central reference of the religious Judaic tradition and in Hebrew means 'instruction'
Twelvers	The largest branch of Shia Islam, *Twelvers* (or Ithna Ashari) refers to those adherents who believe in twelve divinely ordained leaders Imams). Twelvers believe that the last Imam, is hidden from sight and will reappear as the promised Mahdi – an End Times Islamic figure.
Wudu	Ritual purification performed before performing the prayers or reading the Quran
Zabuur	One of the four divine books, the Psalms of David
Zakah / Zakat	Zakah, which is one of the five pillars of Islam, is the giving of alms in accordance with your wealth and according to shariah

CPSIA information can be obtained
at www.ICGtesting.com
Printed in the USA
JSHW030500100321
12403JS00003B/9